COOL FOOD FACTS FOR KIDS

FOOD BOOK FOR CHILDREN

Children's Science & Nature Books

ave you ever wondered how the food as we know it now came to be? We didn't always have fast food restaurants, pizza, or American cheese slices. People survived on different types of food in different countries and different eras. Read further to learn about how people survived in the past.

Native american food.

COOKING AND FOOD IN COLONIAL AMERICA

Colonial Americans would eat various types of food that depended on where they lived and during that era they lived. They fished, hunted game, and grew crops for their food. Many homes would have gardens where they grew herbs and vegetables.

Henry Singleton the Ale-House door c.1790

Ripe corn.

CROPS AND FARMING

As they first arrived in America, corn became one of their more important crops. They learned how to grow corn and make it into cornmeal from the Native Americans. They soon learned how to farm other crops including Squash, Beans, Pumpkins, Oats, Barley, Rice, and Wheat.

The village of native American Wampanoag tribe at Plimoth plantation.

HUNTING

These early colonists and others that lived on the frontier would often hunt for their food. This included Rabbits, Geese, Ducks, Turkey and Deer.

Close up of a Flat Fish in a tidal pool at a beach on Vancouver Island.

FISHING

Many of these colonial towns were near a river or the ocean which provided a good source for food. They ate different types of fish, including Halibut, Lobsters, Clams, Salmon, Trout, Flounder, and Cod.

Small herd of sheep grazing in a field.

LIVESTOCK

They brought domesticated animals with them from Europe that they raised as livestock to use for meat. These animals included Pigs, Chicken, Cattle, and Sheep.

The First Thanksgiving.

WINTER

These settlers had to save their food from the summer and fall to be able to survive winter. They smoked or salted the meat to preserve it. They stocked up on grains, pickled vegetables, and dry fruit so that they would have food for the winter months.

WHAT DID THEY DRINK?

While you might think that they drank mostly milk and water, the water would sometimes make them ill and cows were scarce. Rather, they drank cider, made from peaches or apples, tea, and beer. The kids would also drink watered down beer and cider.

THE DINNER TABLE

Eating dinner at the table was a different experience in colonial times. They would typically stand at the table since there would not be chairs for each person.

They ate with their hands for the most part. The knife was the most utilized utensil.

During the 1700s, wealthy Americans started to eat lavishly. They had access to china, silverware, and chairs for them to sit around the table. They also had access to finer foods including Sugar, Beef, Chocolate, Wine, and Coffee.

Italian Calzone

ANCIENT GREEK FOOD HISTORY

The Ancient Greeks would eat fairly simple foods. Unlike other ancient civilizations, they did not think of rich and extravagant meals as a good thing. Their three basic staples were Oil, Wheat, and Wine.

WHAT MEALS DID THE GREEKS EAT?

They would typically eat three meals a day. Breakfast would consist of a simple and light meal that would usually consist of Porridge or Bread. Lunch would also be a light meal which would also include bread, as well as some Figs or Cheese.

Dinner was the big meal for the day and enjoyed around sundown. It would sometimes consist of a big social event including various foods such as Cheese, Fish, Eggs, Breads, and Vegetables.

TYPICAL FOODS

The Greeks enjoyed simple foods. They would a lot of bread dipped in olive oil or wine. They would also eat a lot of vegetables, including Garlic, Onions, Cabbage, Beans, and Cucumbers. The fruits they enjoyed included Apples, Grapes, and Figs. They would use honey to add sweetness to their foods and to prepare desserts like Honey Cakes.

Fish was the main meat they ate, but the wealthy people would occasionally eat Pork, Lamb, Chicken, and Beef.

Italian antipasti wine snacks set.

DID THEY EAT TOGETHER?

The families would not typically eat together. The women and men ate separately, either at different times or in different rooms. The men often would invite their male friends to dinner and they would drink, eat, talk, and play games for long periods of time. This dinner party was known as a *"Symposium."* Women were not permitted to be a part of this dinner.

WHAT DID THEY DRINK?

The Greeks would drink wine and water. The wine was watered down so that it would not be as strong. Kykeon was a thick gruel they would sometimes drink. It consisted of Herbs, Barley, and Water.

A Kylix was a shallow, large cup they used to drink wine from. Sometimes it included a picture at the bottom which would be seen as the wine was drank from it.

DID THEY EAT ANY STRANGE FOODS?

The Greeks would eat foods that may seem strange today including Locusts, Small Birds, and Eels. The strangest thing might possibly be a popular food for the Spartans named *"Black Soup"* and consisted of Vinegar, Salt, and Pig's Blood.

RENAISSANCE FOOD HISTORY

What did they eat during the Renaissance?

Where people lived and whether or not they were a peasant, or wealthy would designate what type of food they would eat.

Porridge.

PEASANT FOOD

The average person during this time period was considered a peasant. They would eat mush or soup for each meal. These meals would also typically include black bread. The soup consisted of food scraps, usually vegetables like carrots or some eggs. The mush was cooked from some type of grain, like wheats or oats, and cooked in water. Similar to what we know as oatmeal.

They did not get to eat much meat. It was rare and expensive. The meat was hard to get since it needed salt to preserve it. Salt was expensive during this time period. If they were lucky enough to live close to the coast, they would get to eat fish.

FOODS OF THE NOBLES AND MERCHANTS NOBLES

During the Renaissance, the wealthy ate better than the peasants. Similar to the Romans and Greeks which they studied, they were able to enjoy huge feasts consisting of many fancy dishes. They also ate broths and soups like the peasants, but the soups included exotic spices and were often sweetened with sugar.

The rich also enjoyed more meat than the peasants, including pig, stag, and beef roasts. These roasts would be boiled and then would be basted with their juices and rose water for flavor.

FEASTS

Food would get interesting at festivals, weddings, and large feasts. They would often eat big game birds including cranes, peacocks, and swans. After they would clean and cook the birds, they often might reattach its feathers for decoration. These events would include lots of meat like ham, turkey, rabbit, venison, pheasant, chicken, and mutton. The dessert would be referred to as the "Fruit course", and consisted of fruit, nuts, jellies, and cheese.

WHAT DID THEY DRINK?

They did not enjoy water with their meals as we do now, since it would be dirty and not taste good, particularly in the larger towns. People would mostly drink beer (ale) or wine. Wine was more popular in France and Italy, and ale was popular in the areas to the north including England and Germany.

Greek jug on dish.

ANCIENT ROME FOOD AND DRINK

In Ancient Rome, people consumed a variety of foods. What they ate would depend on where they lived and how wealthy they were. Their food was imported from all about the empire so they could feed the number of people in Rome, the capital city.

HOW MANY MEALS DID THEY EAT?

They would typically eat three meals a day. Their first meal, breakfast, was referred to as *"Lentaculum."* It would be eaten at sunrise and would consist of bread and possibly fruit. The second meal, lunch, was known as *"Prandium."* This meal would be very small and consumed around 11 a.m. Their main meal was known as *"Cena"* and was consumed in the afternoon.

WHAT DID THE POOR EAT?

The poor in Rome did not enjoy the same food that the wealthy did. Their main food was porridge which was known as *"Puls"*. Puls consisted of ground wheat and water. On occasion, they would get some fruit or vegetable along with the puls. They did not get to eat much meat.

Porridge.

DINNER PARTIES

The wealthy enjoyed better food than the poor. They often had nice dinner parties which would last for hours and consisted of several meal courses. They enjoyed various foods including cakes, fish, meats, vegetables, eggs, and fruit.

Vegetarian salad with spinach, chickpeas, cherry tomatoes, egg and Feta cheese and lemon.

DID THEY SIT AT THE TABLE?

The Romans would recline on a couch around a table at their formal parties. They laid on their left arm and eat from a table in the center with their right hand. At a less formal meal, they would stand or sit on a stool while they ate.

Couture decadence of Romans.

DID THEY EAT ANY STRANGE FOODS?

At a nicer banquet, they might eat stewed snails, roast peacock, and flamingo's tongues. Dormice, which looks similar to a squirrel, was probably the strangest thing they would eat. It was considered to be a delicacy and would sometimes be enjoyed as an appetizer. One recipe called for it to be dipped in honey and then rolled in poppy seeds.

WHAT DID THEY ENJOY TO DRINK?

The Romans mainly enjoyed drinking wine, even though it would typically be watered down. After learning about how the people long ago ate, aren't you glad you live in today's world where you can have pizza, hamburgers and all the fresh fruit you want?

For additional fun food facts, research the internet, go to your local library, and ask questions of your teachers, family, and friends.

Visit

BABY PROFESSOR
EDUCATION KIDS

www.BabyProfessorBooks.com

to download Free Baby Professor eBooks and view
our catalog of new and exciting Children's Books